# by Jane Manners
# illustrated by
# Dagmar Fehlau

**Harcourt**

Orlando  Boston  Dallas  Chicago  San Diego

www.harcourtschool.com

Janet has some seashells.
She keeps 10 in each jar.

She counts the seashells every day.
How many does she have so far?

**Tim has some marbles.**
**He keeps 10 in each jar.**

4

He counts the marbles every day.
How many does he have so far?

Dad has some pe
He keeps 10 in ea          r.

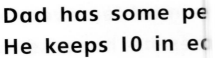

He counts the pennies every day.
How many does he have so far?

Mom has some buttons.
She keeps 10 in each jar.

8

She counts the buttons every day.
How many does she have so far?

Lady has some dog treats.
They make her say "Bow-wow!"

Lady eats some every day.
How many does she have now?

Steve has some jelly beans.
He never knows how many.
He likes to eat them every day,
and soon he won't have any!